GET $mart WITH YOUR MONEY™

Digital Smarts

How to Stay Within a Budget When Shopping, Living, and Doing Business Online

Judy Monroe Peterson

ROSEN
PUBLISHING®

New York

Published in 2013 by The Rosen Publishing Group, Inc.
29 East 21st Street, New York, NY 10010

First Edition

Library of Congress Cataloging-in-Publication Data

Peterson, Judy Monroe.
Digital smarts: how to stay within a budget wh<
doing business online/Judy Monroe Peterson.
    p. cm.—(Get smart with your money)
Includes bibliographical references and index.
ISBN 978-1-4488-8256-4 (library binding)—
ISBN 978-1-4488-8262-5 (pbk.)—
ISBN 978-1-4488-8263-2 (6-pack)
1. Finance, Personal—Computer network resources. 2. Teleshopping.
3. Internet banking. I. Title.
HG179.P44723 2013
 332.024—dc23

                                    2012022099

Manufactured in the United States of America

CPSIA Compliance Information: Batch #W13YA: For further information, contact Rosen Publishing, New York, New York, at 1-800-237-9932.

Contents

Introduction

Buying and doing important business online can be a great idea, but it can also be problematic. Web sites and mobile devices, such as smartphones, can make shopping convenient. People can buy just about any product or service online on computers or smartphones any day, any time. No driving or parking is needed, saving time and money for gas and parking fees. In addition, online shopping often provides a much larger selection of products and services than can be found in any one store locally. Sometimes necessary products are available only online, especially if teens live in remote areas.

Information provided on Web sites can help people learn more about products. Teens can compare brands and features and read reviews about a product or a seller. Usually, online products are ready to be purchased and can be shipped immediately. By doing research online, shoppers may discover lower prices for items than they would find in a local store. Buying online sometimes reduces the total cost of an item because customers may not have to pay sales tax.

Shopping and doing business online can also pose disadvantages. For example, shipping and handling fees may increase the cost of products purchased online and delivered to

Computers and mobile devices allow for instant online shopping with credit cards. Shoppers can use all-purpose cards such as Visa, MasterCard, and Discover at thousands of online stores.

the home. In some cases, buying the items at local stores may be a better deal. In addition, states are increasingly passing laws to collect sales tax from online retailers.

Online shopping can be fun and practical when people keep their budget in mind and stick to it. To avoid financial problems and make better buying decisions, teens should decide in advance exactly what they need and what they can afford. Digital resources are available to help young people set up and maintain a budget. Teens can use a combination of high- and low-tech strategies for money transactions such as paying bills or investing. Many people find that managing finances online is quick and convenient. Like buying products online, electronic financial services are typically available twenty-four hours a day. Personal finance and budgeting software may be purchased or downloaded for free from a variety of reputable open-source sites.

CHAPTER 1

Shopping at Online Stores

Getting a good deal online is more than getting the lowest price on an item. Smart shopping online requires knowledge. Shoppers need to know the vendors they are doing business with and understand the information provided about products. Teens should have an idea of what they want before shopping online. They need to set a budget before shopping and stick to it.

Buying online has some disadvantages. People cannot do hands-on inspection of products or try on merchandise such as clothes, shoes, or jewelry. They cannot talk face-to-face with a seller or salesperson. Other issues can arise, including late delivery of items, shipment of wrong or damaged items, and hidden fees. Teens should know the quality expected of the product or service, promised arrival time, warranty, return policy, and if the company provides support for questions or problems.

Steps to Buying Online

Although every site is a little different, selecting and paying for an item through a computer or

7

People can consult with friends and family members to find useful and reliable Web sites for shopping and doing business.

a smartphone is similar. To find a product, people type key-words in a Web browser such as Google Chrome, Safari, Firefox, or Internet Explorer. Then they click on the links that display possible Web sites for buying the desired item. Sometimes people go directly to a company's site to shop. There, they can read information about products and see prices.

When shoppers choose an item, they click on a button such as "Buy," "Add to Cart," "Add to Bag," or "Add to Basket." The item is put into an online shopping cart, bag, or basket. Then they can continue shopping or begin to check out.

At checkout, buyers can review their cart or bag to make sure the items and quantities are correct. Then they complete one or more pages of forms with information such as their name, e-mail address, street address, phone number, and shipping instructions. Entering payment information and any promo or coupon codes is next. Buyers usually have options for paying, such as with a credit card or through PayPal. Services like PayPal securely store all payment information for people, including their bank account or credit card numbers. Buyers can then pay or send money without showing their financial information to others.

Once an order is placed, a confirmation page appears with an order or reference number and purchase details. A confirmation is also sent to the e-mail address provided during checkout. Teens should save this information on their computer or smartphone or print it. They may need it if problems with shipping occur or other questions arise.

Comparison Shopping

One benefit of shopping online is the ability to research a product before buying or deciding not to buy. Doing research can help people determine the best price for an item and if the seller is trustworthy. Shoppers can access various sources for product reviews. Amazon is widely used by people to post and read product reviews. Retailers' sites may have reviews of their products or services. Another way to research products is to use sites that offer or collect reviews. With just a click, people can turn to sites such as Buzzillions and Epinions to see what others have to say about a product.

Teens might want to go to several sites to shop because no one site has the best deal every time. Some sites, such as Shopping.com and PriceGrabber.com, provide tax and shipping costs along with the product's price. Other comparison sites are BizRate, Shopzilla, and BeatMyPrice. Specialized

Shopping in Stores with Smartphones

Smartphone applications (apps) combine in-store shopping with online information. In-store shoppers can look
up reviews and prices by scanning the bar code of a product with their smartphone. Apps such as Price Check,
TextBuyIt, RedLaser, and ShopSavvy provide price and
discount comparisons. With some apps, people can speak
the product name into their smartphone or snap a photo
of a product to find more information. People using

Using bar code apps for smartphones, such as this one from ShopSavvy,
shoppers can search the Internet for reviews and price comparisons on a
store's products.

ShopSavvy can scan for prices and see if an item is available online or in local stores. Other apps like Slifter, TheFind, and Pic2shop compare prices of items at local stores. Consumer Reports Mobile, a mobile Web site, gives people with smartphones access to the Consumers Union's product reviews, ratings, and comparisons of products and services. This independent organization does not accept advertising.

online shopping directories can be useful for finding electronics, clothing, shoes, or sporting goods all in one place.

Coupons and Social Couponing

Coupon codes can impact final costs when shopping online. People can search for a store along with keywords like "discount," "coupon," "coupon code," "promo code," or "free shipping" to find available discounts.

Social couponing gives people group purchasing power to get deep discounts on a variety of products and services. Sellers offering group coupons hope to attract new customers to try their products or services. They also hope people will share the information with family and friends via e-mail, Facebook, or Twitter. To use social couponing, people sign up at a Web site and receive coupon or voucher offers every day, which they can print and redeem (use). Deals are usually offered for a short period of time, such as one day. Groupon, LivingSocial, Scoutmob, and Crowd Cut are all sites that provide group deals. Some city news sites also have local group coupons.

Group couponing sites offer coupons or vouchers with reduced prices on a variety of products and services. People can subscribe to daily deals e-mails through free member sites such as Groupon.

Social coupons may offer large discounts on clothing, shoes, household items, cultural events, restaurants, sporting goods, and services for cars and other vehicles. Unlike using regular coupons, consumers must pay for the item (such as a dinner for two) up front in order to take advantage of the deal. Some coupons or vouchers must be used right away, while others have a longer expiration date.

Groupon requires a specific number of people to commit to buying a deal before the discount goes into effect. The deal is canceled if not enough people buy it, and credit cards are not charged. LivingSocial offers a deal every day with deep discounts at local restaurants, theaters, and more. Scoutmob sends group deals to smartphones.

Impulsive and Compulsive Purchasing

It can be tempting to make impulsive purchases when shopping online. People may find it difficult to resist a good deal, particularly if a store highlights a discounted item for a limited time. Sometimes they buy more products or services online than they budgeted for or spend more than they planned. Or they may forget about purchases because the items can take days or weeks to arrive.

Small costs can pile up fast. A song or movie may cost a dollar or two, but some people impulsively download hundreds in a short time. People might sign up for online music or movie subscriptions that are automatically charged to their credit card or bank account every month. However, they might not remember the services or know how to cancel them. Although one service might cost $10 a month, multiple services add up.

Some people can become compulsive shoppers. Compulsive shoppers regularly buy too many unnecessary things. The appeal of compulsive shopping is the process of searching out and obtaining a new or better item. These shoppers find the process so exciting that the desire to buy overrides their spending plans. This can leave them deep in debt.

Both impulsive and compulsive buyers may experience financial stress when their credit card bills are due. Some may have used debit cards to buy merchandise with money from their bank accounts. As a result, they may not have enough money to buy necessary items, like gas or car insurance, or pay their rent and utility (water, heat, and electricity) bills.

Teens can take steps to rein in impulse buying. When shopping, it's important to weigh needs versus wants. After putting an item in an online shopping cart, teens can walk away before ordering it and think about what else their money

Young people can avoid getting buried under a mountain of debt by using credit cards wisely. People have too much debt if their use of credit is regularly near or over their limit.

is needed for. This can help them cool off and decide if they really should buy the item. Turning off shopping alerts helps curb impulse buying. Converting monthly costs of automatic subscriptions to an annual cost is one way to see the impact on a budget clearly. Teens who stick to their budgets tend to avoid overspending and acting impulsively or compulsively.

Rights When Shopping with Online Companies

The Federal Trade Commission (FTC) requires online companies to follow rules. Companies must ship an item within the time promised. If no delivery time is stated, they must ship within thirty days of receiving an order. Another rule requires businesses to notify customers if an item cannot be shipped on time. Customers can then choose to wait or cancel the order and get a refund. After canceling, money must be refunded within seven days or credited within one billing cycle if charged on a credit card.

Once purchases are received, customers have the right to return a defective item and get their money back. Also, companies often allow the exchange of clothing, shoes, and other items to get a correct fit. For exchanges of an online purchase, people may have to pay for the return shipping, in addition to the original shipping costs.

Sometimes people receive an item and decide they do not want it. The company's policy determines if store credit or a refund is issued. Not all stores allow returns. If they do, stores differ in their policies and may charge fees for return shipping or restocking an item. Even if an online store accepts returns, it may issue refunds only by the method of payment or by giving customers credit to buy other items at the store. For these reasons, shoppers should carefully read the return and cancellation policies on a company's site before buying.

Using Online Auctions, Classified Ads, and Swaps

A popular way to buy online is through auctions, classified ads, and swaps. Teens might find good deals or unusual items using these sources. Smart shoppers first research the value of an item. Then they establish a top price and plan to stick to it before placing an auction bid or contacting someone about a classified ad.

Methods of Payment

Teens need to know how to pay for something before buying on a computer or mobile device. Auction sites like eBay and others require members to be at least eighteen years old. A person under eighteen can use an adult's account with the permission of the account holder. However, the account holder is responsible for everything done with that account, including paying for a winning bid.

Sellers choose which type of payment to accept. Some limit buyers to credit cards only. A safe way to use credit cards is to sign up with an online payment service such as PayPal or Noca.

PayPal and similar services redirect customers to an online payment site to complete a transaction. In this way, people can buy items from various Web merchants but keep their card numbers private.

Some credit card companies also offer this feature. By using an online payment service, buyers never have to show credit or bank information to online businesses or individuals. The seller pays any fees for use of the online payment services.

Some online sellers accept money orders, cashier's checks, personal checks, or cash. Do not use these forms of payment online. Using credit cards provides protections to buyers that money orders and checks do not. People should never send cash through the mail for their purchases. Cash can be easily stolen and is hard to track down if lost.

Popular Online Auction Sites

Major online auction sites include eBay, uBid, WebStore, Online Auction, and Auction-Warehouse; eBay is probably the best known. People can find almost anything on eBay, such as clothes, household and sporting goods, jewelry, furniture, and even vehicles! People looking for items in a particular category such as computers, electronics, art, or collectibles may want to go to sites that auction only those specific items.

Online Auctions

Using Internet auction sites can be a good way to buy and sell goods or services. These sites are convenient because they can be accessed day or night. Some offer a huge variety of new and used items from around the world. People may find lower prices on items than they would when shopping at online or local stores. At some sites, the seller must sell all items at the price of the lowest successful bid. Other sites allow the seller to get the highest price that is bid.

Online auction sites often allow sellers to set a reserve price. This means the seller will not sell the item below that price. The sites indicate that a reserve price exists but do not show the reserve price to bidders. To win the auction, a bidder must meet or exceed the reserve price and be the highest bidder. The seller and highest bidder do not have a sale if the reserve price is not met. Sometimes people use

People new to online auctions need to read the auction companies' guides carefully. Each auction site has its own set of rules to follow.

reverse auction sites such as Oltiby.com to enter details of what they want to buy. The reverse auctioneer forwards their request to other sites. A match may or may not be found.

Buying at Online Auctions

Auction sites vary as to their rules. On most sites, people need to register and choose a username and password. People can use the site's search tool to browse categories and look for a specific item. They can also enter keywords into the search tool to find a product or seller.

19

Many online auction sites provide step-by-step instructions for people to learn how the bidding process works.

Once an item is found, bidders should carefully read the information on the page. They need to pay attention to the product's description, the seller's terms and conditions, and the payment and shipping methods. Other important information includes the seller's satisfaction rating and buyer feedback. Smart customers learn about any protections they may have, such as free insurance, guarantees for items not delivered or returned, or recourse if the item is not what the seller claimed. Sellers should be willing to answer any questions about their auction items and terms. It is a good idea for bidders to make electronic or print copies of all transaction information.

Many auction sites have two ways to buy an item—by fixed price or bidding. A fixed-price item is usually marked with the phrase "Buy It Now" or something similar. By clicking this button, the bidding process is bypassed, and the item is placed in the buyer's cart. People can continue to shop or check out.

Clicking "Place Bid" or a similar button begins bidding. Beforehand, people need to determine their budget for the item and make sure they really want it. They should also set a top price and stick to it. Placing a bid is a legal contract (commitment) to purchase an item.

Proxy bids are a common way to make an initial bid and set a maximum one. People's bids are automatically increased against competing bids until they win the auction or someone outbids their maximum.

After the auction closes, the highest bidder is the winner and is responsible for promptly paying the seller. If the winners do not pay, they have violated their contract and can be kicked off the auction site forever.

Each auction site has its own rules for cancelling a bid during an auction. Most provide a form for bidders to cancel and correct their bid price. Sometimes the item description is changed and bidders no longer want it. People should think carefully about canceling a bid because this information appears on their feedback numbers. This can cause sellers to block them from future bidding.

Online Classified Ads

Using online classified ads is another way to buy products and services. When buyers see an item they want, they contact the site, which uses e-mail to put them in contact with the sellers. Buyers and sellers can exchange e-mails or agree to meet. Large classified ad sites include Craigslist, Kijiji, and BackPage. They offer the convenience of shopping day or night, and sellers can keep the ads up-to-date. These general sites offer free ads, except for some real estate and job ads. Other smaller classified ad sites focus on specific items, such as books, clothes, computers and electronics, cars, antiques, or collectibles.

Most online ads are posted on Craigslist, which has sites for cities small and large all over the world. The ads on Craigslist are local. This means the buyer and seller can choose to meet in person to complete the deal. In this case, the buyer does not pay for shipping, and the seller may not need an online payment service. However, teens should exchange goods in this way only with the help and supervision of an adult. If the item is costly, both the seller and buyer may want to sign an agreement about their transaction.

Before buying anything on a classified site, people will want to read the site's terms and conditions and any safety tips, and they should understand how to report abuse. Buyers should never include a personal phone number when responding to an ad. It is best to deal with local people and meet face-to-face at a public place like a coffee shop, fast-food restaurant, or local library. Teens should bring a parent or other trusted adult to the meeting. Buyers should carefully check over the item

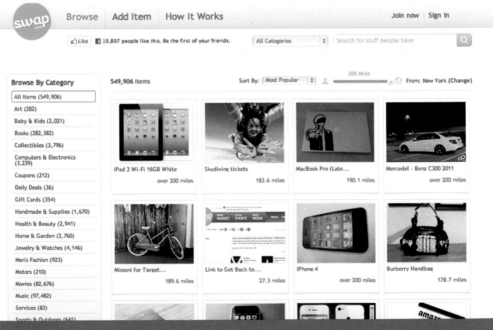

Teens new to online swapping might want to use sites like Swap.com (http://market.swap.com) that have been around for a while, show new listings each day, and can confirm the activity on their site.

before paying for it. If the item is a computer or other electronic item, plug it in or try it out to make sure it works.

Online Swaps

People use online swapping to trade goods or services like snow shoveling, lawn mowing, or dog walking in exchange for things they want. They may be able to get lightly used items for free or just for the cost of shipping. There are a variety of swaps, reuse directories, and materials exchange sites. Some sites offer free exchanges or bulletin boards. Others charge a user fee.

A popular trading site is Swap.com. People worldwide use it to swap books, DVDs, music, video games, clothing, and many other things. Peerflix offers a one-stop trading site for all DVD needs. Lala provides a trading service for music, and Goozex deals solely in games. For teens who want to trade books, CDs, and DVDs, Title Trader and PaperBackSwap might prove to be useful sites. People turn to Zunafish for bartering and trading both goods and services.

Myths & Facts

Myth　It is best to make buying decisions based solely on online customer reviews.

Fact　Customer reviews are only opinions and may provide useful insight into the contents of items or how they work. Although they can help as purchasing guides, people should make buying decisions based on their budget, needs, wants, personal taste, and quality of the product.

Myth　An online auction bid can be cancelled if a better price is found at another online auction.

Fact　Finding the same item for a lower price does not count as a reason to cancel a bid.

Myth　People can get their money back for digital gift cards that they lose.

Fact　Some financial institutions and companies issue prepaid electronic gift cards, telephone cards, and mass transit passes. Most digital gift cards are not covered if lost or misused.

Chapter 3

Digital Money Tools: Banking and Bill Paying

Using online banking sites and personal-finance software can help people organize and manage their money and keep spending within a budget. Everyday tasks or complex calculations can be completed quickly and easily. Teens may feel more in control of their finances when managing them digitally. As a result, they may stay within a budget, which can help reduce spending and increase saving.

Banking Options

Virtual (Web-based) banks and most brick-and-mortar (physical) banks offer online services. The Federal Reserve System, the Federal Deposit Insurance Corporation (FDIC), and federal banking agencies regulate both types of banks. Virtual banks provide many of the same services as regular banks. However, people cannot walk in and do face-to-face transactions with tellers or bankers. People can go in person to physical banks. Wells Fargo, Bank of America, Citibank, U.S. Bank, and other large banks have branch offices across the country. Local community banks are also widely available.

Customers may have fewer surprises when using online banking compared to traditional paper-based banking because they can check their balances and transactions at any time from a computer or mobile device.

Most virtual and regular banks post a lot of information on their Web sites about their accounts and services. Using a computer or smartphone, teens can research and compare the services of different banks and credit unions. Credit unions are nonprofit financial institutions owned by the people who use them. Like banks, they are regulated by the federal government.

Banks and credit unions offer many kinds of accounts, including checking accounts. They usually charge fees for their different checking accounts and other financial services. Basic or low-activity accounts often require people to pay a small monthly fee and maintain a minimum balance. Free checking accounts are sometimes available, but they usually do not pay interest and they may have fees for certain services.

Some banks require teens to open an online joint checking account with a cosigner, such as a parent or guardian. If a problem occurs with the account, the cosigner will assume responsibility. Other banks have special checking accounts for students. Teens usually do not pay a monthly fee, but they may have some limitations in using the account.

Using a Bank's Online Features

Many people find online banking to be a useful tool for following their budget and tracking money. They can access their account at any time, and they do not need to fill out paper forms to do money transactions. Once they log in to their account, people can check the balance, transfer money between accounts, view statements, and pay bills. Account information can be downloaded to personal-finance software like Quicken, AceMoney, Bank Tree Personal, or iCash. Banks may or may not charge fees for their online services.

To use a bank's online features, customers fill out an application and choose a username, password, and personal identification number (PIN). They also sign an official signature authorization form. The bank keeps customers' signatures on file to prevent fraud. Finally, people make a deposit to open the account. They can now go to the bank's site and log in with their username or number and password. Every site differs, but online banking information usually looks like printed bank statements. It shows deposits (money added) and withdrawals (money taken out) of an account. On many sites, clicking a link next to a check number displays a picture of the canceled check.

More banks and credit unions are offering mobile check deposits.
Customers use their smartphones to take pictures of paper checks to
deposit money.

Some people pay bills and buy products with personal
checks. Many merchants now process checks electronically.
In a store, paper checks are run through an electronic system
that sends information from the check (not the check itself)
to a bank or other financial institution. The funds are then
transferred into the store's account. Customers get a copy of
the signed receipt for their records. They also get their check
back, which is marked and cannot be used again. Similarly,
many companies and individuals now digitally send information on checks to banks to transfer funds into their accounts.
An overdraft penalty is charged if not enough money is in
the account to cover a check.

Online Money Transfers

With online banking, people can move money instantly between accounts at the same bank. Teens might deposit their paycheck into a checking account and then transfer some of it into their savings account to earn interest. Then they can move money from savings to checking when making payments for things they need, such as car repairs. Most banks handle transfers on the same business day, or the next day if the transfer occurs after a cutoff time. For example, some banks process transfers on the same day if they are made before 3:00 PM.

Many banks allow people to make electronic transfers to and from accounts at other banks. However, the transferred money may take two to seven days to show up. Most banks charge a fee for transfers between banks.

Online Bill Paying

Most banks and credit unions provide online bill paying. This service is often free and can save people money because they do not need to buy checks, stamps, and envelopes. Instead, they go online and authorize the bank to transfer money from their account to pay bills. People can use this method for one-time payments or recurring payments (for example, payments that occur once every month). Using online bill paying can help give people a greater sense of control over what gets paid and when.

To set up electronic bill payment service, people log in to their checking account and go to "Bill Pay" or something similar. They choose the companies to pay. If a company is not listed, customers can enter the account number and the name and address. Then, whenever they need to, they can go to

Processing Electronic Money Transfers

Most online money transfers are processed through the Automated Clearing House (ACH) network. This electronic-funds transfer system uses computer technology instead of paper checks and forms. ACH is used for payroll direct deposits; e-checks; credit cards and debit cards; payments for rent, loans, and insurance premiums; and federal and state tax payments. When a bank sends payment for a bill, the company receives an ACH transfer or a paper check. ACH transfers are fast and reliable, although not all companies use this feature. The company usually receives the payments the next day, and the funds are moved almost instantly. Paper checks issued by a bank are mailed through the U.S. Postal Service and take longer to arrive.

their bank account, choose a company, and enter the amount to pay and the date. The bank moves the money out of the account and transfers it to the company on the specified date.

Many people like the convenience of a bank's automatic bill paying service for routine monthly bills. They use it to pay their rent, auto and insurance payments, cell phone bills, and more. Many banks offer this service for free, but others charge a fee. Using automatic bill paying ensures that bills are paid on time and for the correct amount. This feature can save people time and worry about paying their bills on time. To set up the service, people tell the bank which bills they want to pay automatically. Then the bank takes money from their checking account to pay the same amount monthly on a specified day of the month.

Issues When Paying Bills Electronically

People may run into problems when paying bills online. For example, they might continue to make automatic payments for products and services they no longer want or need. Forgetting about the payments or finding it easier to do nothing, they continue to get charged. Teens should review their bills every month and decide whether their ongoing payments

Automatic payment plans can make it easy to forget what gets paid each month and when. Keep a paper or online calendar as a reminder to check for regular bill payments.

fit their budget. Another reason to check online bills and accounts regularly is to watch for errors and report them to the bank right away. When people switch checking accounts, they need to reset their automated bill payments. People must also update their automatic payment information if a credit card account expires or is closed and reopened with a new number.

If teens spend more money than they have in their account, the bank issues an overdraft notice and charges a fee. This can be costly because the bank charges for each check or transaction that cannot be paid. The bank also returns the electronic or paper check to the company, which often adds its own fee. To avoid piling up these penalty costs, teens can keep extra money in their checking account. They also need to remember to subtract the amount for each paid bill from their account balance. Some banks offer automatic e-mail reminders when bills are due. People can also use their computers or smartphones to create automatic reminders.

Another way to avoid extra fees is to sign up for overdraft protection. This electronic service links a person's checking and savings accounts. If not enough money is in the checking account to pay a bill, the funds are pulled from the linked savings account.

Chapter 4
More Digital Money Tools

A variety of digital tools are available to help people manage their money. Some are free. Others must be purchased. Online or software programs can make keeping track of money easier, whether money is going into or out of an account.

Credit Cards

Banks and other financial institutions issue credit cards. These plastic cards allow people to borrow money for buying clothing, gas, online movies and music, concert tickets, and many other things. Credit is a temporary loan, and the money must be repaid. A very high rate of interest is charged if the entire credit card bill is not paid in full by the due date.

People can search online to compare different credit card offers before signing up for one. Many credit cards include conveniences such as the ability to check balances and recent transactions online and download account information into personal finance programs. Consumers can use Web sites like Bankrate.com, Consumer-action .org, CardWeb.com, and CardRatings.com to compare credit card services and fees.

Credit cards can be helpful in handling one-time, unexpected expenses, such as emergency car repairs.

Sometimes a special low interest rate is offered at sign-up. Be aware that the rate may end in a few months and a higher one may go into effect. People get penalties (they are charged extra fees) if they pay their bill late or charge more than their credit limit. Their interest rate may also go up. If possible, try to find a credit card that has no annual fee and a low interest rate on the amount owed.

By using credit cards wisely, young people can establish a good credit history. In turn, this can help them get auto loans, student loans for college, and home loans. There are some good reasons to use credit cards. Buying online and in local stores with a credit card is usually easier and safer than paying by check. Checks include information a thief could use to access an account. Sometimes people pay by credit card for a large, unexpected expense, such as car brakes that suddenly go out. Using credit can help people manage such purchases if their emergency fund is low. People may also charge an item to take advantage of a sale and then pay later.

However, credit cards can make impulse buying and overspending easy. Cardholders need to be careful not to spend more than they can afford to pay back. If just the minimum required payment on a credit card bill is made, most of the money goes to pay interest or finance charges. Not much is left to pay the principal, or the original amount borrowed. People may end up spending much more than the item's original price.

Overcharging can lead to major debt problems and a poor credit report. This can limit one's ability to get loans for cars or school or renting an apartment. Some employers even cancel job opportunities after discovering a candidate has a poor credit record.

Debit Cards

Both debit cards and credit cards let people spend money without having to carry cash. Using them to buy products is fast and easy. The two types of cards have important differences, though. A debit card is linked to a checking account. When making a purchase with a debit card, money is electronically taken out of the checking account and immediately transferred to the store's account. Banks may charge an annual fee for a debit card or a small fee for each transaction.

With their debit card and a personal identification number, people can electronically withdraw cash from their checking account at an automated teller machine (ATM). Withdrawals occur immediately. Banks may limit how much money can be taken out in a twenty-four-hour period. At ATMs, people can also make deposits or transfer funds between accounts.

Many banks charge a fee every time a debit card is used at another bank's ATM. These fees can add up quickly. Sometimes people use their debit card and accidentally spend or withdraw more than they have in their account. The bank may pay the overage but will charge the customer a large penalty.

Electronic Savings Accounts

Banks and credit unions pay customers interest for using the money they deposit in savings accounts. In turn, this encourages people to save. These accounts are safe places to hold money that is not needed right away. The federal government insures accounts up to $250,000 at banks and credit unions through the Federal Deposit Insurance Corporation. Interest rates can vary over a period of time and for different accounts. A bank's Web site can be used to view account

Electronic Investing and Trading

Young people may want to grow their money by digitally investing in and trading stocks, bonds, and mutual funds. Investing online may save money and time. Online brokers and major mutual fund companies offer competitive online services. They may do this by eliminating costs for branch offices and by accepting and processing trades by computer. However, inexpensive

Online investing allows people to see real-time activities affecting their investments.

electronic investment companies may have limited products and services and may not offer the best mutual funds. Reaching real people to ask for help may be difficult. Online trading might save transaction costs. However, it may encourage people to trade more than they should, resulting in higher total costs and lower investment returns. In addition, people may be tempted to shift funds around and try to play all the angles. This can swamp smart financial management. Steady growth and long-term investments and savings are preferable to daily wheeling and dealing.

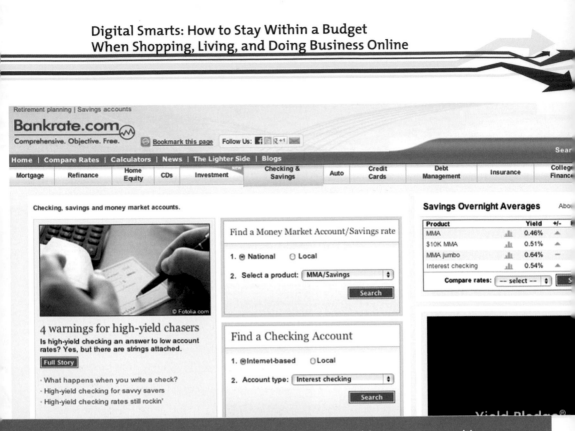

Bankrate.com (http://www.bankrate.com) provides consumers with current rates on credit cards, auto loans, money market accounts, certificates of deposit, checking and ATM fees, and online banking fees.

information and transfer funds between accounts. Also, savings account information can be downloaded to personal finance software.

Teens can do research online and compare savings accounts. Most banks have a Web site where they post savings options and interest rates. Compounding is key to saving because interest can be earned on savings and on the interest the money earns. Teens will want to find out how much interest is paid and when. Interest may be paid daily, monthly, quarterly, or yearly. This impacts the amount of interest earned. Even 1 or 2 percent interest paid on money in a savings account can make a big difference in the long term. To compare rates at local banks or around the country, the federal government recommends using Bankrate.com.

On the Web, teens can find out the minimum amount a bank requires for customers to open a savings account. They will also want to determine how easy it is to put money in and take money out of a bank's savings account. Banks usually charge a fee when a savings account balance falls below a minimum amount. Fees vary from bank to bank.

Managing Money Digitally

Online tools and personal software can help teens stick to a budget or spending plan. Personal finance programs help people see how they spend, save, and invest their money. They can then decide if they need to make changes to meet their spending and saving goals. It does take time to learn how to use these programs and keep them up-to-date.

Many banking sites allow customers to link to online accounts at other banks, credit unions, credit card companies, and financial institutions. Money can be tracked at any time by computer or smartphone. Most banks provide this service on their Web site, usually at no charge.

Similar programs are offered by non-bank Web sites, such as Mint and Yodlee Money Center. These sites provide free tools and advice to help people with budgeting. Some have chat rooms where ideas about money can be shared with other members. When people log in to their accounts on these sites, all of their transactions are pulled together. They can view their spending, pay bills, and transfer funds. They can see how much money goes to buy gas and pay for rent, entertainment, or eating out. Financial information on these sites and online banking sites is password-protected and kept safe by security technology.

Some people use online tools or personal finance software to pay bills and track money going into and out of their accounts. Others set up spreadsheets. Find a method that works well for you.

Another way to track money digitally is to enter spending and other financial information into computer software. Smartphone apps are also available for this purpose. People can track and manage their savings, investments, debts, and loans. They can also use word processing or spreadsheet software to set up a money management system.

One reason teens may want to use money management tools is to make sure they have funds to cover their current purchases and to pay for future college and emergency expenses. To do this, they need to keep accurate records of the dates and amounts of checks and debit card purchases. They can keep copies or access electronic versions of bank account and credit card statements. It is important to save ATM and deposit slips, canceled checks, and any receipts for purchases. Teens also need to make sure they record all transactions in their checkbook register.

Ten Great Questions to Ask a
FINANCIAL ADVISER

1 What online services are available to help me learn how to budget money and pay bills?

2 How much time will it take me to plan and set up a budget online or with computer software?

3 How many credit cards and online bank accounts should I have?

4 I scheduled an automatic payment online but then changed my mind. What should I do?

5 How am I protected if someone steals and then uses my credit card or debit card?

6 Should I use my credit card, debit card, or bank account number to prove my identity?

7 Some Web sites that provide free budgeting tools carry advertising for buying things online. Can I trust these ads?

8 Should I be investing money online? What are the best online investments for me?

9 Rates for a car loan at a Web-only bank and a brick-and-mortar local bank may be different. Why?

10 What information do I need to save from digital and paper account statements?

CHAPTER 5
Protecting Money Digitally

The Internet provides people with easy access to a huge range of products and services to buy. There are downsides to this convenience, however. Sometimes teens fall for online scams and lose money. Purchases and other online experiences may not be private because some companies collect and sell information about who buys what, where, and how. Teens can take many steps to protect themselves while shopping and doing business on computers, smartphones, and other mobile devices.

Preventing Online Fraud, Scams, and Spams

One of the best guidelines to follow when shopping online is to know the seller. People can research a seller by going to the business's Web site and looking for a section called "About Us." State and local consumer offices may have information about a company. Some online sellers are members of programs such as the Better Business Bureau (BBB). Companies that carry the BBB Accredited Business seal for the

The Web site of the Better Business Bureau (http://www.bbb.org/us) offers timely information for consumers, including details on retail stores, products, and services; rip-offs and scams; and digital and financial safety.

Web have been checked out by the BBB. However, this seal is not a guarantee of a seller's good business practices. The BBB site provides ratings (with letter grades A, B, C, D, or F) to show if a company is reliable and willing to resolve customers' concerns.

Dangers of Phishing

Phishing is a fast-growing Internet crime. It is the use of e-mail to steal important personal information, such as credit card numbers, passwords, PINs, Social Security numbers, and driver's license numbers. Thieves may use the information to steal a person's identity or empty a bank account. Although these e-mails are phony, they often seem real. They may claim to come from a bank, credit card, eBay, or other online account. The e-mail says the account has problems and instructs the receiver to click on a link to verify his or her personal information. Never click on these links. Legitimate companies do not ask for passwords, account numbers, or other such personal information by e-mail. Instead, teens should contact the business directly by typing the company's Web address into a browser and finding the "Contact Us" or similar section.

Another way to find out about online sellers is to search for consumers' comments. Using a search engine, enter a company's name and a term such as "review," "rating," "scam," or "complaint." Teens can also read buyers' ratings of online stores at Bizrate.com. Some auction sites such as eBay post ratings of sellers based on buyer comments.

An offer that seems too good to be true is probably a scam. Perhaps the seller came by the items illegally, or the item is damaged but is not advertised as such. If something goes wrong with an online purchase, people should find out whom to contact. They may need to talk to their bank or credit card company or an authority such as the Federal Trade Commission. Federal law protects credit card holders if disputes with a seller come up or if fraudulent (false) charges are made on the card.

Spam e-mail may contain phony offers for products or investments that could end up costing time and money. Many spam messages include a link to unsubscribe from their e-mail lists. People should not click on any links or reply to messages in a spam e-mail. If they do, they could be put on other spam lists. Most e-mail programs have built-in spam filters. A separate program that filters spam and moves suspicious e-mail to a spam or junk folder can also be installed. Reporting spam can help an e-mail provider track and reduce spam for everyone.

Protecting Online Privacy

The Internet is a convenient place to purchase things, transfer money, pay bills, renew driver's licenses, and do other business. However, personal information can be stolen online. To help protect privacy, people can look for and read privacy statements on Web sites. It's important to make sure companies do not sell details about customers to other companies. Policy statements are usually found on companies' Web sites in the "About" or "FAQ" section. The policies explain how information is collected and protected.

People will want to stick with secure Web pages when doing online transactions. These sites encrypt (scramble) personal information to make it difficult to change or steal. One signal of security is an unbroken key or a closed lock to the left of the Internet address or on the bottom of a Web page. Another signal of a secure site is that the first letters of the

Internet address are "https." If a site is secure, the likelihood of identity theft is usually low.

Spyware is often put onto computers and smartphones as people browse the Internet. These programs track what people do when they are online. Tracking can help companies figure out how to use advertising to sell things to consumers. For example, if someone searches for "movie reviews," an ad might pop up for a new movie coming to theaters soon. Sometimes spyware is used to steal passwords and other personal information. To help with this problem, an anti-spyware program can be installed and run regularly.

Identity Theft

Identity theft is when someone steals and illegally uses a person's name, credit card number, Social Security number, or other personal information. Thieves might use the information to sign up for cell phone services and run up large bills, open credit card accounts and buy many costly items, or take out a loan. The National Crime Prevention Council estimates that identity theft happens to millions of people every year, and about one-third of the victims are between eighteen and twenty-nine years old. Teens are at high risk because they frequently use the Internet and share personal information on blogs and social networking sites such as Facebook and Myspace.

People need to be careful about identity theft because they are responsible for any debts in their name. They may have trouble getting credit cards and even driver's licenses due to bad credit histories. Many hours of hard work—and sometimes thousands of dollars in legal fees—may be needed to restore a damaged credit history.

Reduce the risk of identity theft by tearing up or shredding credit card offers, account statements, unwanted receipts, and other financial documents before throwing them away. At ATMs, people should use their free hand to block others from seeing the keyboard when entering their PIN. When using a computer or smartphone, teens should be careful to keep others from seeing their personal information.

Teens should not tell their password or PIN to anyone, not even a friend. It is smart to avoid family or pet names, common words, telephone numbers, birthdays, and other information that may be easy to guess when creating passwords. Someone who guesses a password may be able to log in to accounts or pose online as that teen. The longer the password, the tougher it is to crack. For PINs, an address, telephone number, Social Security number, or birth date should not be used. A password or PIN should be changed if one suspects that someone else knows it.

Report identity theft immediately. Call the financial institution at the phone number on the account statement or on the back of the credit or debit card. Any accounts the thief used should be closed. Next, report the fraud to the local police and keep a copy of the police report in a safe place. Victims can file a report with the Federal Trade Commission as well. They can also place a fraud alert with one of the three credit reporting bureaus: Equifax, Experian, or TransUnion.

Individual Responsibility

Many people use the Internet to shop and handle financial matters. Every time customers are asked to provide personal information—whether in an online form, e-mail, text, or phone message—they need to decide if they can really trust the request. Each person must protect his or her money.

People want to be careful about storing and displaying personal information online. For example, they should not

Do not let anyone near you watch your ATM transactions. Sometimes people offer to help with a machine that appears not to work correctly, but they are really memorizing the customer's PIN.

store their credit card information on Web sites and apps. When using smartphones, people can limit the amount of personal information stored in the device. They can also use the "key lock" function so that others cannot access their smartphone. When a computer is not in use, lock it. People should avoid doing financial transactions on public Wi-Fi, offered in some libraries, stores, coffee shops, and other places, because personal information is not protected. Teens can limit who can access their social networking profiles and create different lists of people who can view their posted information.

When using ATMs, people need to be alert to their surroundings and prevent others from seeing their PIN.

Free public Wi-Fi hotspots are convenient for laptop, smartphone, or tablet users. However, people should avoid doing online shopping or banking there: the public network may not be secure.

Memorize PINs; do not write them down. People should avoid carrying their PIN or Social Security number in a wallet, purse, or backpack.

An important money protection step is to monitor banking and credit card accounts regularly. This can help teens find unusual purchases or activities, which they should check out right away. Also, teens need to compare the bank's records to their own records to make sure they agree. If there is a problem, they should contact the bank as soon as possible.

Following these guidelines will help teens manage their money online and keep their personal information safe. This will allow them to enjoy the convenience of shopping, budgeting, and managing their money online now and in the future.

Glossary

automated teller machine (ATM) An electronic machine that performs basic banking functions, such as withdrawals and deposits.

budget A plan for how to use one's money.

chat room A virtual room where people have online interactive discussions.

checking account A bank account that allows a person to take out money, pay bills, or buy things by writing checks or making withdrawals.

comparison shopping The practice of researching products and services to buy the highest quality at the lowest price.

compound interest Interest that is earned on an amount of money (usually savings), as well as on the accumulated interest on that money.

cosigner Someone who acts as a joint signer, guaranteeing payment if the primary signer does not make payments.

credit An agreement in which someone buys something now and promises to pay for it later.

credit card A plastic card issued by banks, stores, and other businesses that allows the cardholder to buy products and services on credit. Credit cards charge interest, usually beginning one month after a purchase is made.

credit history A record of an individual's past borrowing and repaying.

debit card A plastic card used to withdraw money directly from a checking account or to make payments electronically without having to write a check.

debt An amount of money owed to another party, usually after having borrowed it.

emergency fund An amount of money set aside to be used in an emergency, such as the loss of a job, an illness, or another large, unexpected expense.

fraud The crime of using deception for personal financial gain.

identity theft The theft and use of a name, Social Security number, credit card number, or other personal information for illegal purposes.

interest A charge paid for the use of borrowed money.

investing The act of committing money to an asset, such as stock, property, etc., in order to make a profit in the future.

loan A sum of money borrowed for a certain amount of time.

overage An amount by which a transaction (such as a withdrawal or a payment) is too much.

overdraft fee A penalty payment for having a negative balance in an account.

recourse An opportunity to use or do something in order to deal with a problem.

savings account A bank account in which money is deposited for safekeeping and earning interest at a modest rate.

spreadsheet program Computer program that arranges information, often financial data, in a table, chart, or graph.

statement A summary of account activity issued by banks, credit card companies, or other financial institutions.

transaction A transfer of money from one account, person, party, etc., to another. Withdrawals and deposits are typical transactions at banks and other financial institutions.

Wi-Fi A wireless networking technology that uses radio waves to provide a wireless high-speed Internet connection.

For More Information

Canadian Bankers Association (CBA)
Box 348
Commerce Court West
199 Bay Street, 30th Floor
Toronto, ON M5L 1G2
Canada
(800) 263-0231
Web site: http://www.cba.ca
The Canadian Bankers Association provides information for
teens to learn about money, budgeting, credit, invest-
ments, and banking in Canada.

Consumer Federation of America (CFA)
1620 I Street NW, Suite 200
Washington, DC 20006
(202) 387-6121
Web site: http://www.consumerfed.org
The Consumer Federation of America is an advocacy, research,
and education organization providing information on
personal finances, including money management and
budgeting.

Council for Economic Education (CEE)
122 East 42nd Street, Suite 2600
New York, NY 10168
(800) 338-1192
Web site: http://www.councilforeconed.org
This organization provides a personal finance Web site for
teens at http://www.italladdsup.org, which covers budgeting, credit, saving, and investing.

Federal Deposit Insurance Corporation (FDIC)
550 17th Street NW
Washington, DC 20429-9990
(877) ASK-FDIC [275-3342]
Web site: http://www.fdic.gov
The FDIC protects individuals against the loss of deposits. This
   agency also provides information on shopping for financial services, understanding consumer rights, and
   avoiding financial fraud.

Federal Trade Commission (FTC)
600 Pennsylvania Avenue NW
Washington, DC 20580
(202) 326-2222
Web site: http://www.ftc.gov
The Federal Trade Commission works to prevent fraudulent,
   misleading, and unfair business practices in the market-
   place and to provide information to help people spot,
   stop, and avoid them.

Financial Literacy and Education Commission
1500 Pennsylvania Avenue NW
Washington, DC 20220
(888) MY-MONEY [696-6639]
Web site: http://www.mymoney.gov
The Financial Literacy and Education Commission offers information from various federal agencies on money
   management and budgeting.

Financial Planning Standards Council (FPSC)
902–375 University Avenue
Toronto, ON M5G 2J5

Canada
(800) 305-9886
Web site: https://www.fpsc.ca
The Financial Planning Standards Council provides information
        for teens on personal finance, budgeting, savings, invest-
        ments, and more.

Institute of Consumer Financial Education (ICFE)
P.O. Box 34070
San Diego, CA 92163
(619) 239-1401
Web site: http://www.financial-education-icfe.org
The Institute of Consumer Financial Education is a nonprofit
        public education organization that promotes wise credit
        use, saving, and investing.

Jump$tart Coalition for Personal Financial Literacy
919 18th Street NW, Suite 300
Washington, DC 20006-5517
(888) 45-EDUCATE [453-3822]
Web site: http://www.jumpstart.org
Jump$tart offers information on money management, budget-
        ing, credit, investing, and savings. Go to its clearinghouse
        to find a list of books and other print materials, CDs,
        DVDs, videos, and Web sites.

Web Sites

Due to the changing nature of Internet links, Rosen Publishing
has developed an online list of Web sites related to the subject
of this book. This site is updated regularly. Please use this link
to access the list:

http://www.rosenlinks.com/GSM/Digi

For Further Reading

Butler, Tamsen. *The Complete Guide to Personal Finance: For Teenagers and College Students*. Ocala, FL: Atlantic Publishing Group, 2010.

Butler, Tamsen. *The Complete Guide to Your Personal Finances Online: Step-by-Step Instructions to Take Control of Your Financial Future Using the Internet*. Ocala, FL: Atlantic Publishing Group, 2011.

Cindrich, Sharon Miller. *A Smart Girl's Guide to the Internet: How to Connect with Friends, Find What You Need, and Stay Safe Online* (Be Your Best). Middleton, WI: American Girl Publishing, 2009.

Holmberg, Joshua, and David Bruzzese. *The Teen's Guide to Personal Finance: Basic Concepts in Personal Finance That Every Teen Should Know*. New York, NY: iUniverse, 2008.

Hoole, Gavin, and Cheryl Smith. *The Really, Really, Really Easy Step-by-Step Guide to Online Buying & Selling: For Absolute Beginners of All Ages*. London, England: New Holland, 2009.

Kamberg, Mary-Lane. *Frequently Asked Questions About Financial Literacy* (FAQ: Teen Life). New York, NY: Rosen Publishing, 2011.

Kristof, Kathy. *Investing 101*. Updated and expanded ed. New York, NY: Bloomberg Press, 2008.

Lawrence, Judy. *The Budget Kit: The Common Cents Money Management Workbook*. 6th ed. New York, NY: Kaplan Publishing, 2011.

Minden, Cecilia. *Smart Shopping* (Real World Math: Personal Finance). Ann Arbor, MI: Cherry Lake Publishing, 2008.

Monteverde, Matthew. *Frequently Asked Questions About Budgeting and Money Management* (FAQ: Teen Life). New York, NY: Rosen Publishing, 2009.

Orr, Tamra. *Privacy and Hacking* (Cyber Citizenship and Cyber Safety). New York, NY: Rosen Central, 2008.

Peterson's. *Don't Break the Bank: A Student's Guide to Managing Money*. Los Angeles, CA: Peterson's, 2012.

Saddleback Educational Publishing. *Budgeting & Banking Math* (21st Century Lifeskills Mathematics). Costa Mesa, CA: Saddleback Educational Publishing, 2011.

Saddleback Educational Publishing. *Smart Shopping Math* (21st Century Lifeskills Mathematics). Costa Mesa, CA: Saddleback Educational Publishing, 2011.

Sandler, Corey. *Living with the Internet and Online Dangers* (Teen's Guides). New York, NY: Facts On File, 2010.

Bibliography

Benson, April Lane. "Don't Shop, Swap! Redux." *Psychology Today*, May 31, 2011. Retrieved January 3, 2012 (http://www.psychologytoday.com/blog/buy-or-not-buy/201105/dont-shop-swap-redux).

Bickle, Marianne. "The Economic Benefit of Rising Gas Prices." *Forbes*, February 21, 2012. Retrieved February 22, 2012 (http://www.forbes.com/sites/prospernow/2012/02/21 the-economic-benefit-of-rising-gas-prices/?feed=rss_home).

Consumers Union of U.S., Inc. "23 Tips All Online Shoppers Should Know." *ShopSmart*, April/May 2009. Retrieved January 4, 2012 (http://www.shopsmartmag.org/files/23_online_shopping_tips.pdf).

Federal Deposit Insurance Corporation. "FDIC Consumer News Winter 2008/2009—Special Edition: Managing Your Money in Good Times and Bad—When the Economy Cools Down, Financial Scams Heat Up." May 24, 2010. Retrieved January 3, 2012 (http://www.fdic.gov/consumers/consumer/news/cnwin0809/scams.html).

Federal Deposit Insurance Corporation. "FDIC Consumer News Winter 2009/2010—Online Banking, Bill Paying and Shopping: 10 Ways to Protect Your Money." February 19, 2010. Retrieved January 3, 2012 (http://www.fdic.gov/consumers/consumer/news/cnwin0910/online_banking.html).

Federal Deposit Insurance Corporation. "Taking Control of Your Finances: A Special Guide for Young Adults." Spring 2005. Retrieved January 4, 2012 (http://www.fdic.gov/consumers/consumer/news/cnspr05/index.html).

Federal Trade Commission. "Electronic Banking." April 23,
     2010. Retrieved January 3, 2012 (http://www.ftc.gov/bcp
     /edu/pubs/consumer/credit/cre14.shtm).
Fiegerman, Seth. "Impulse Buys: The Real Risk of Online
     Shopping." MainStreet.com, February 9, 2011. Retrieved
     January 5, 2012 (http://www.mainstreet.com/article
     /smart-spending/impulse-buys-real-risk-online
     -shopping?page=3).
Gordon, Rachel Singer. *Point, Click, and Save: Mashup Mom's
     Guide to Saving and Making Money Online*. Medford, NJ:
     CyberAge Books, 2010.
Karp, Gregory. *The 1-2-3 Money Plan: The Three Most
     Important Steps to Saving and Spending Smart*. Upper
     Saddle River, NJ: FT Press, 2009.
Lynn, Jacquelyn. *Online Shopper's Survival Guide: Order
     Anything, Anywhere, Anytime*. Irvine, CA: Entrepreneur
     Press, 2006.
National Consumers League's Fraud Center. "General
     Merchandise Sales." 2009. Retrieved January 22, 2012
     (http://www.fraud.org/tips/internet/merchandise.htm).
National Crime Prevention Council. "Teens: Protect Your
     Identity from Thieves." 2012. Retrieved February 22, 2012
     (http://www.ncpc.org/programs/teens-crime-and-the
     -community/publications-1/preventing-theft/contact).
New York Department of Sanitation, Bureau of Waste
     Prevention, Reuse and Recycling. "NYCWasteLess:
     Online Reuse and Material Exchanges—Products and
     Services." 2012. Retrieved January 6, 2012 (http://www
     .nyc.gov/html/nycwasteless/html/resources/prod_serv
     _general_exchanges.shtml#individual).
OnGuardOnline.gov. "Computer Security." September 2011.
     Retrieved February 9, 2012 (http://www.ftc.gov/bcp/edu
     /microsites/onguard/articles/computersecurity.shtml).

OnGuardOnline.gov. "Spam." September 2011. Retrieved January 3, 2012 (http://www.ftc.gov/bcp/edu/microsites /onguard/articles/spam.shtml).

Perry, Sue. "Cool New Shopping Tools for 2012." *ShopSmart,* January 17, 2012. Retrieved January 20, 2012 (http:// www.shopsmartmag.org/2012/01/cool-new-shopping -tools-for-2012.html).

Shinder, Debra Littlejohn. "Money Matters on Your Smartphone." TechRepublic.com, December 19, 2011. Retrieved January 3, 2012 (http://www.techrepublic.com /blog/smartphones/money-matters-on-your-smartphone /3987?tag=rbxccnbtr1).

Tyson, Eric. *Personal Finance for Dummies.* 6th ed. Indianapolis, IN: Wiley Publishing. 2010.

U.S. Department of Justice. "What Are Identity Theft and Identity Fraud?" 2012. Retrieved February 20, 2012 (http://www.justice.gov/criminal/fraud/websites/idtheft.html).

Index

About the Author

Judy Monroe Peterson holds two master's degrees and is the author of numerous educational books for young people. She is a former technical, health care, and academic librarian and college faculty member; a research scientist; and curriculum editor with more than twenty-five years of experience. She has taught courses at 3M, the University of Minnesota, and Lake Superior College. Currently, she is a writer and editor of K–12 and post–high school curriculum materials on a variety of subjects, including life skills.

Photo Credits

Cover (right) © iStockphoto.com/Diana Hirsch; cover, p. 1 (top left) © iStockphoto.com/Tolga Sipahi; cover, p. 1 (center left) © iStockphoto.com/sturti; cover, p. 1 (bottom left) © iStockphoto.com/Alekseenko; cover, p. 1 (background) © iStockphoto.com/Dean Turner; pp. 4–5 Jamie Grill/Iconica/Getty Images; pp. 7, 16, 20, 25, 33, 43 Jason Reed/Ryan McVay/Photodisc/Thinkstock; p. 8 Ron Levine/The Image Bank/Getty Images; pp. 10, 11, 18, 24, 30, 37, 45 (boxed text backgrounds) © iStockphoto.com/Michael Monu; p. 12 Bloomberg/Getty Images; p. 14 George Doyle/Stockbyte/Thinkstock; p. 17 Jose Luis Pelaez Inc./Blend Images/Getty Images; p. 19 © iStockphoto.com/Trevor Smith; p. 26 Comstock/Thinkstock; p. 28 Vstock LLC/Getty Images; p. 31 Image Source/Getty Images; p. 34 Diego Cervo/Shutterstock.com; p. 37 Stephen VanHorn/Shutterstock.com; p. 40 Steve Cole/Digital Vision/Getty Images; p. 42 © iStockphoto.com/Vasiliy Kosyrev; p. 49 LianeM/Shutterstock.com; pp. 50–51 John Lund/Marc Romanelli/Blend Images/Getty Images; interior page graphics (arrows) © iStockphoto.com/Che McPherson.

Designer: Sam Zavieh; Editor: Andrea Sclarow Paskoff;
Photo Researcher: Karen Huang